MIND GRENADES

I DON'T KNOW ABOUT YOU,

HARDWIRED

MIND

GRENADES

DESIGN AND EDITORIAL DIRECTION BY JOHN PLUNKETT AND LOUIS ROSSETTO

MANIFESTOS

FROM THE

FUTURE

HardWired

520 Third Street

Fourth Floor

San Francisco

California 94107

BUT I HATE READING INTRO-

First Edition 1996

Printed in Singapore

10 9 8 7 6 5 4 3 2 1

ISBN 1-888869-00-3

Book design by
John Plunkett.

Credits appear in the

back of the book.

DUCTIONS.

I always figure the work should speak for itself, which is why I don't write an editor's page for *Wired*. Instead we start each issue with a graphic statement–a "mind grenade"–to prepare readers for the visual and intellectual assault to come. In *Wired* shorthand, we call this section the Intro Quote.

When creative director John Plunkett and I first sat down to discuss *Wired,* we decided it should focus not on technology but on remarkable people, and that it should feel as exciting as the times we are living through. And we agreed that it should look like it had fallen out of the sky, off another planet. If you stumbled across it in the street, you'd be compelled to pick it up; and even if you didn't understand it, you would instinctively sense that it was smart and cool–that you had to invest the energy to figure it out. The Intro Quotes are part of that strategy.

Additionally, we wanted to have our own homage to one of our favorite books, Marshall McLuhan and Quentin Fiore's *The Medium Is the Massage.* Indeed, the first Intro Quote, in *Wired*'s premiere issue, was the first paragraph of that book.

I pick the Intro Quote by looking at all the stories going in an issue and trying to find the one quote that feels like a manifesto from the future, something that could be carved into the side of a public building. I then pass it on to John, who figures out how to communicate the idea visually. Then he contacts the designer, photographer, or illustrator who will actually execute our vision. Usually it takes a good two to three weeks of intense back and forth to get it right. Over these past few years, we have worked with an exceptional group of people, who have done, as this book demonstrates, unparalleled work.

The Intro Quotes are where all of us stretch artistically and techno-logically, making full use of the most modern desktop capabilities and digital prepress technologies, and of Danbury Printing & Litho's 6-color Harris Heidelberg M-1000 web press (most magazines use 4-color presses). And, reproducing the first three years of *Wired*'s Intro Quotes in a single volume– *Mind Grenades: Manifestos from the Future*–has led us to push the technology even further, printing this book with 25 match colors, eight over eight on each press form.

Not surprisingly, some critics grumbled that if they had access to all that technology and used fluorescent inks, they too could make *Wired*. So in January 1995, we decided to produce a black and white issue (see 3.01)– to prove the founding premise: that the excitement is not about technology, it's about extraordi-nary people doing amazing work. **Anyway, this is about all the intro-**duction to the Intro Quotes any-body should be forced to read. In the end, this work doesn't speak for itself–it fairly shouts.

Louis Rossetto
Editor/Publisher, *Wired*
San Francisco

"**The medium,**

or process, of our time – electric technology –

is reshaping and restructuring patterns of social interdependence

and every aspect of our personal life.

It is forcing us to reconsider and re-evaluate practically

Everything is

every thought, every action, and every institution

formerly taken for granted.

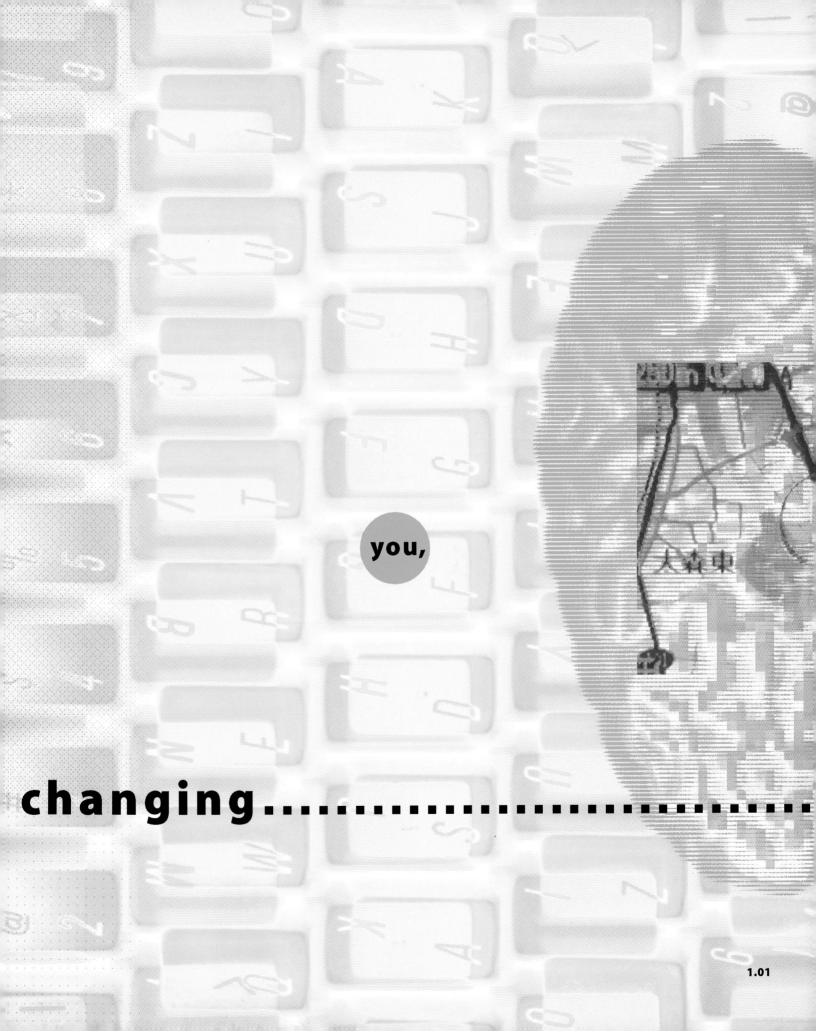

you,

changing...

your education,

your family,　　　　your neighborhood,

your job,

your government,

And they're chang

your relation to "the others."

1.01

Why Wired?

Because the Digital Revolution is whipping through our lives

like a Bengali typhoon – while the mainstream media is still groping for the snooze button.

And because the computer "press" is too busy churning out the latest

PCInfoComputingCorporateWorld iteration of its ad sales formula cum parts catalog

to discuss the meaning or context of **social changes so profound** their only

parallel is probably the discovery of fire.

There are a lot of magazines about technology.

Wired is not one of them. *Wired* is about the most powerful people on the planet today –

the Digital Generation. These are the people who not only foresaw how the merger

of computers, telecommunications and the media is transforming life at the cusp of

the new millennium, they are making it happen.

Our first instruction to our writers: Amaze us.

Our second: We know a lot about digital technology,

and we are bored with it. Tell us something we've never heard before, in a way we've never

seen before. If it challenges our assumptions, so much the better.

So why now? Why *Wired*? Because in the age of information overload,

the ultimate luxury is meaning and context.

Or put another way, if you're looking for the soul of our new society

in wild metamorphosis, our advice is simple. Get *Wired*.

– LR

ng dramatically." Marshall McLuhan

The Medium is the Massage 1 9 6 7

"The message is that all information providers will be in a common business –

the bit radiation business – not radio, TV, magazines, or newspapers."

of the leap

"The suddenness   **to software**

from hardware

"12 percent of the US adult population admits to being physically addicted to television."

"If nothing else, Europe's failures [in technology policy] should provide lessons

from which the Americans can learn.

The worry, however, is that America will not learn."

cannot but produce

"If everyone encrypts, there certainly would be a weakening of our intelligence agencies,

a period of anarchy

and possibly our national security."

and collapse,

"What follows from imagining a Knowledge Machine

is a certainty that School will either change very radically or simply collapse....

The possibility of freely exploring worlds of knowledge

calls into question the very idea of an administered curriculum."

"Video suffers from a deeper problem,

one of ever diminishing reliability in the face of ever more capable morphing

especially

technologies. By decade's end, we will look back at 1992 and wonder how a video of police beating a citizen

could move Los Angeles to riot."

NEO-NAZIS: SACHA HARTGERS–FOCUS-MATRIX. MADONNA: MARC MORRISON/SHOOTING STAR. YELTSIN: KLAUS REISINGER–BLACK STAR. BUSH: GERALD SCHUMANN–PICTURE GROUP. IRAQI WOMEN: GREGORY HEISLER/THE IMAGE BANK. FACING PAGE: EBN/TVT RECORDS.

in the developed countries." – Marshall McLuhan

"**Life in cyberspace** is more **egalitarian** than elitist,

more **decentralized** than hierarchical…

...it serves individuals and **communities,** not mass audiences...

1.03

"International economic theory is obsolete.
The traditional factors of production - land, labor and capital -
are becoming restraints rather than driving forces.
Knowledge is becoming the one critical factor of production."
– Peter Drucker

"Promoting progress in the arts does not inherently
justify the idea that authors are entitled to any particular sort
of copyright, or even that copyright should exist at all."
– Richard Stallman

"A 1990 Harris poll on privacy found that about 79 percent
of those interviewed were 'very concerned' that some aspect
of their private lives is threatened every day."
– Brock Meeks

...We might think of life in cyberspace as

shaping up exactly like

Thomas Jefferson

would have wanted it: founded on the primacy

of individual liberty

and a commitment to pluralism,

diversity, and community."

– Mitchell Kapor

"Abandoning people and products is the necessary handmaiden of
organizational survival. In the early '70s, the last round of military cuts
in the California Bay Area caused massive unemployment; but
that became the fertile ground in which Silicon Valley blossomed."
– Peter Schwartz

"The computer culture has learned from
human interface research that the most supreme form
of interaction is the lack of it: Less is more."
– Nicholas Negroponte

"I want to discuss another **dinosaur,** one that may be on the road to **extinction.**

I am referring to the American **media...**

And I use the term extinction **literally.**

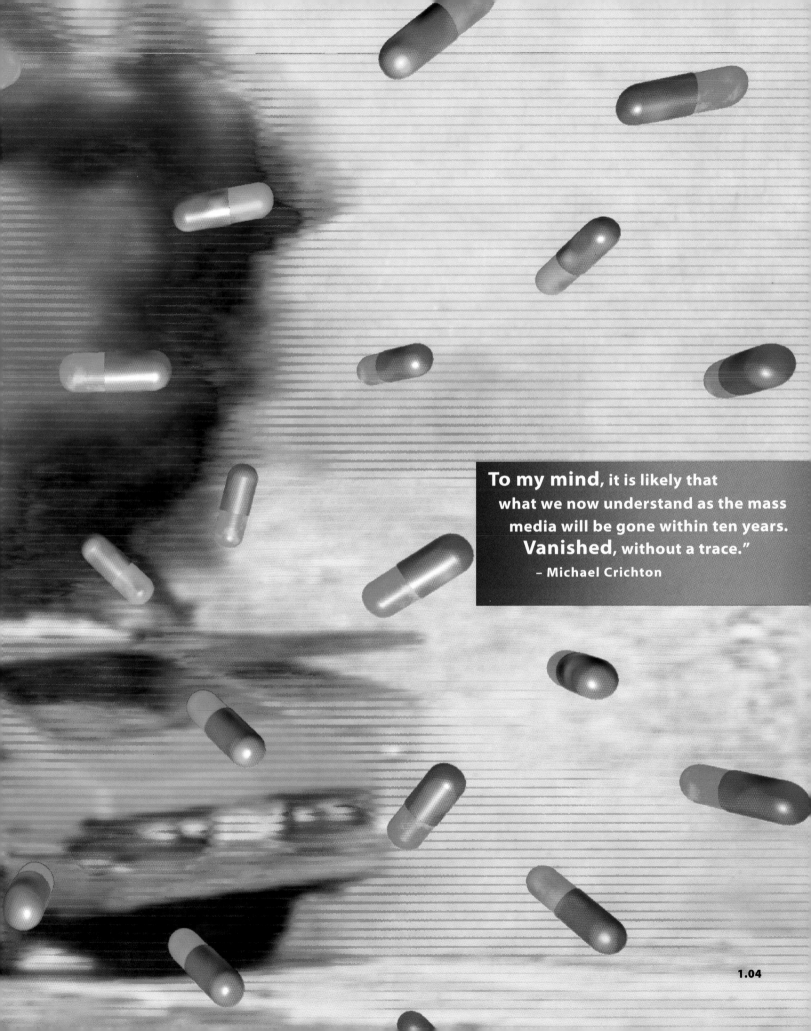

To my mind, it is likely that what we now understand as the mass media will be gone within ten years. **Vanished,** without a trace."
– Michael Crichton

"If you look at the **marketplace,**
we go from **mass distribution and mass markets**
to **micro markets.**

If you look at **family structure**, we go from everybody in the nuclear family to a **multiplicity of forms.**

1.05

And if you look at **war,** we're going to niche economies and **niche warfare."**
– Alvin Toffler

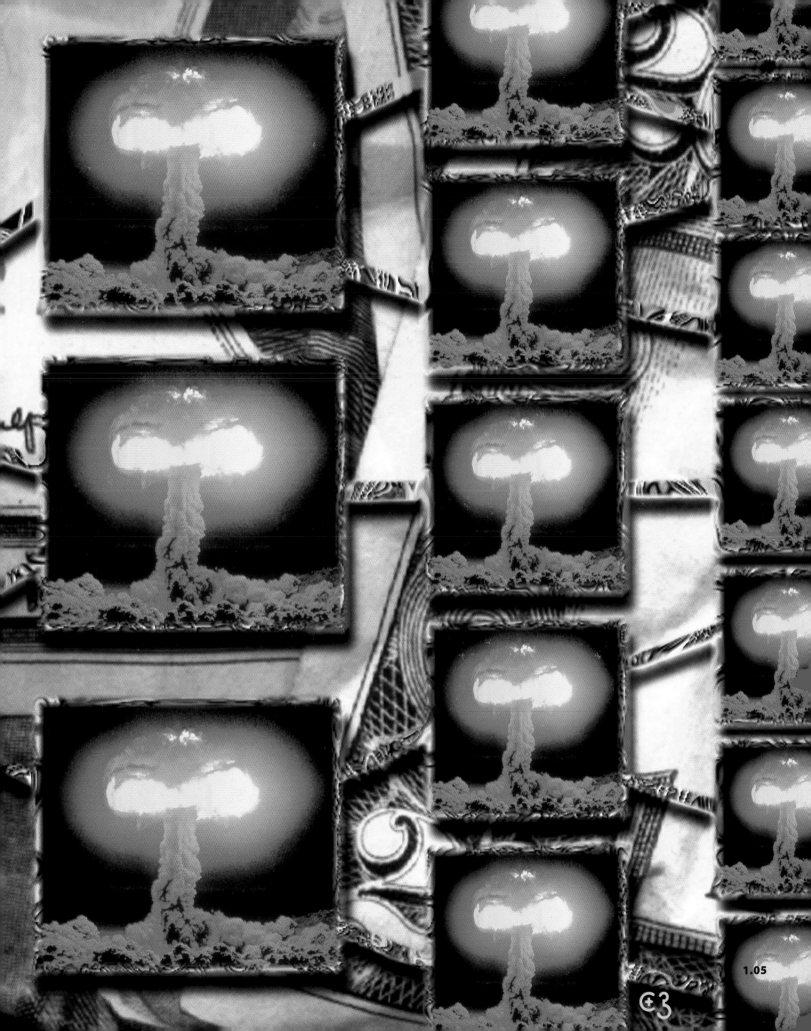

1.05

"Immersive technology on the **one** and on the **other** hand, the beacon that draws creative toward the culmination of represents,

hand,

the grail at the end of the history of

cinema,

Fig. 1.0

energies

computing...

1.06

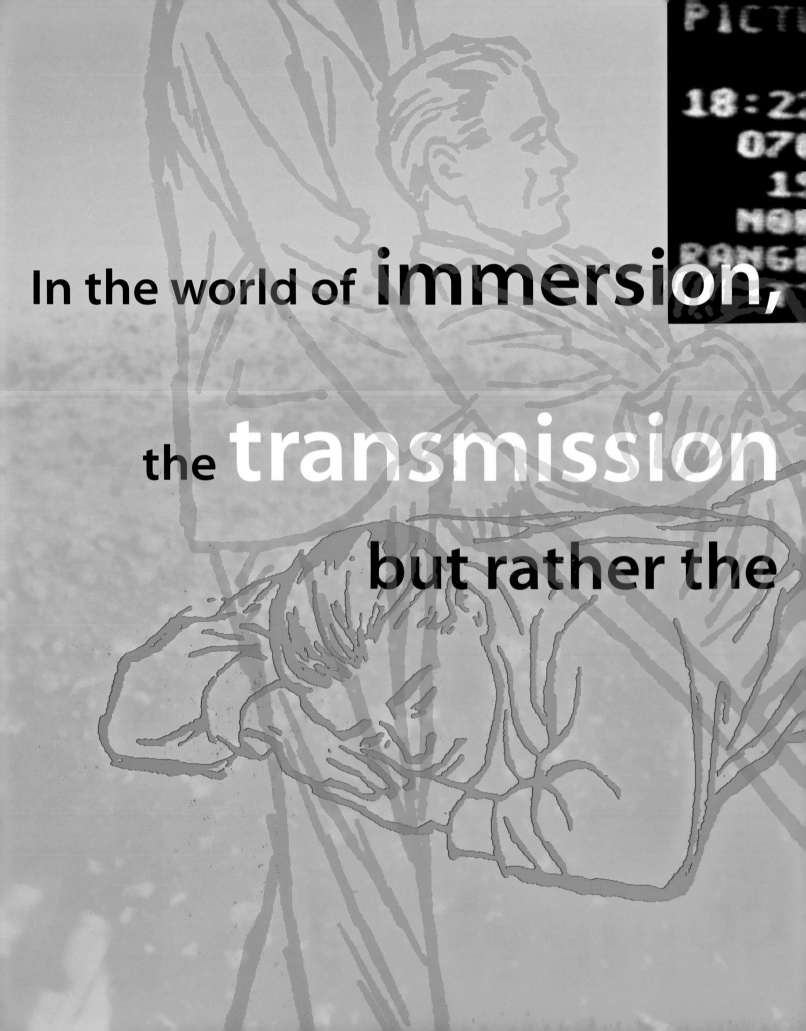

In the world of immersion, the transmission but rather the

authorship is no longer

of experience,

construction

of utterly personal experiences."

– Brenda Laurel

1.06

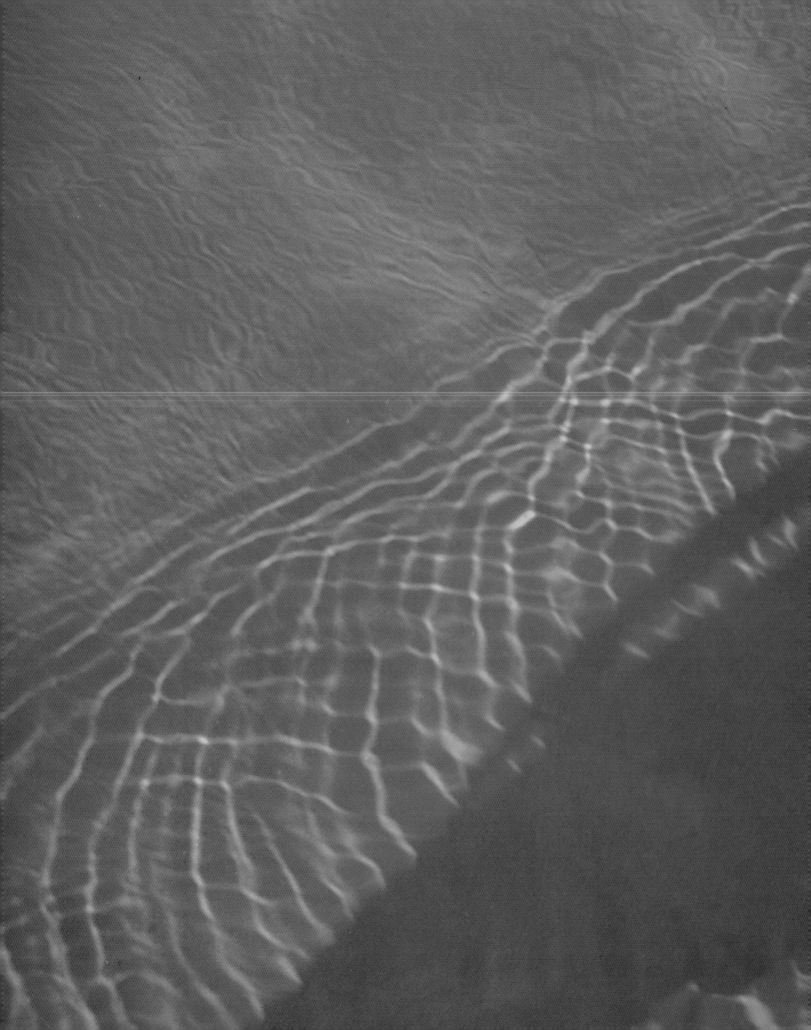

1.06

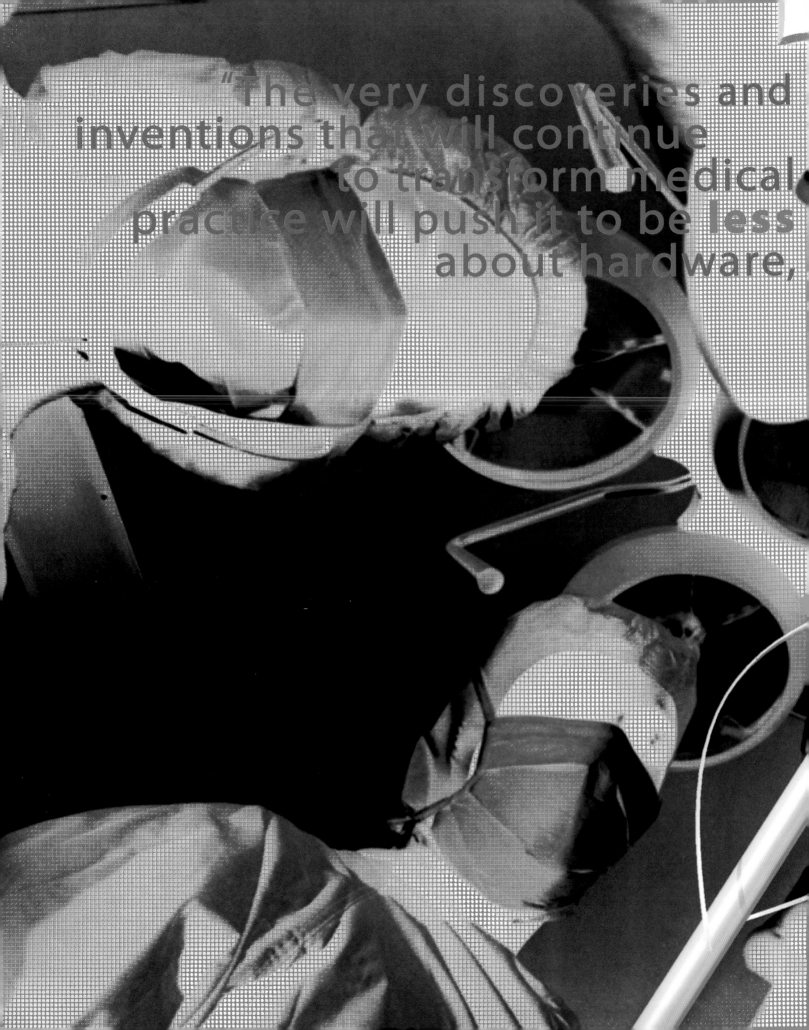

"The very discoveries and inventions that will continue to transform medical practice will push it to be less about hardware,

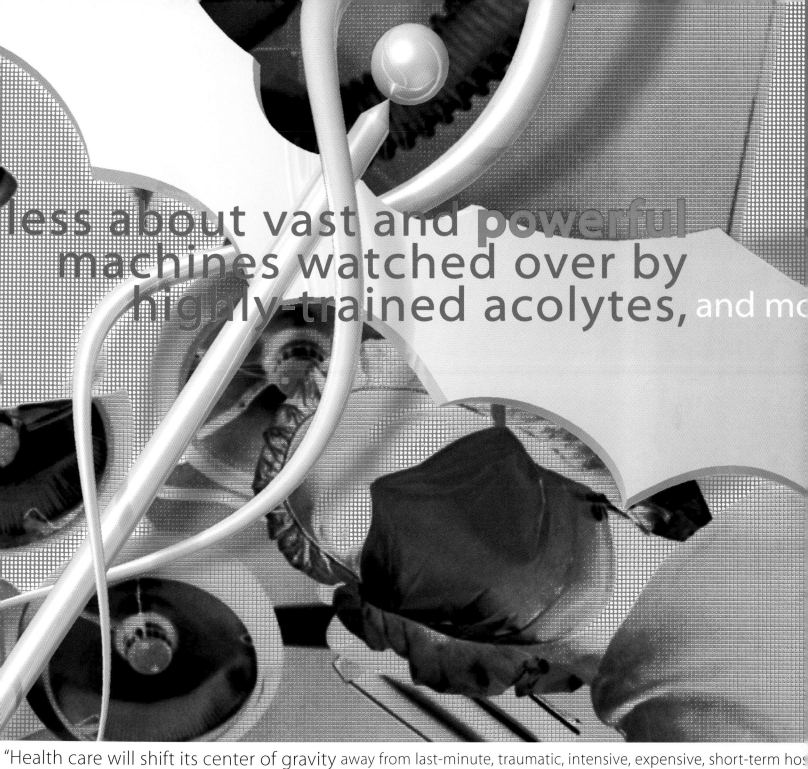

less about vast and **powerful** machines watched over by highly-trained acolytes, and mo

"Health care will shift its center of gravity away from last-minute, traumatic, intensive, expensive, short-term hos

ore about shared information."

ospital-centered care, **and toward early-as-possible, preventive application of information**

n the community and the family."

Joe Flower

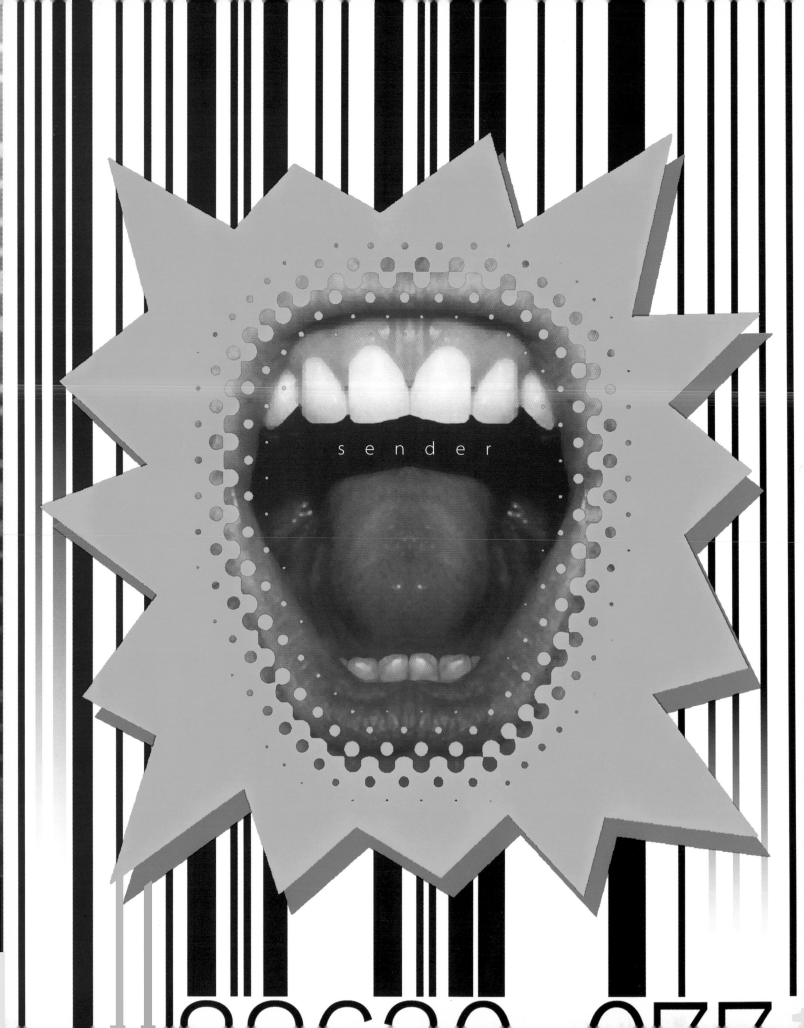

sender

"The fashionable, faux futurism predicts that this time will be different, that this time new media technology will guarantee the individual the upper hand over the advertiser. More likely, we'll see these new media renegotiate the power between individuals and advertisers . . .

INTER

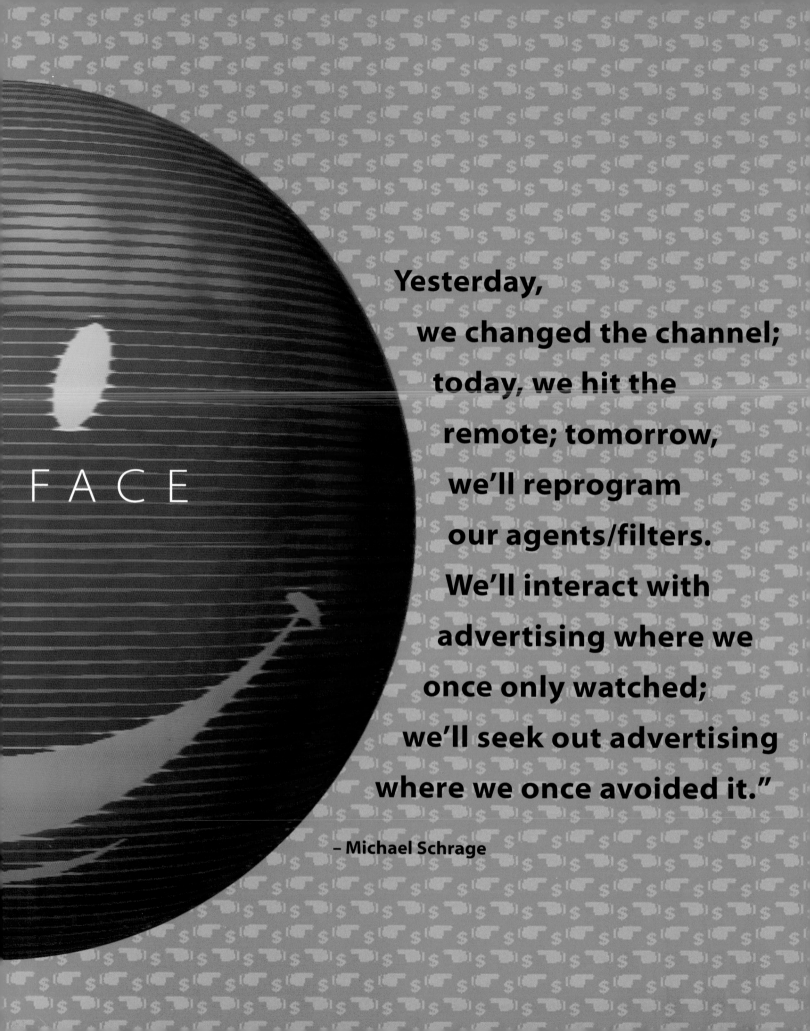

FACE

"Yesterday,
we changed the channel;
today, we hit the
remote; tomorrow,
we'll reprogram
our agents/filters.
We'll interact with
advertising where we
once only watched;
we'll seek out advertising
where we once avoided it."

– Michael Schrage

receiver

Content

*All the goods of the Information Age —
All of the expressions once contained
in books or film strips or records or
newsletters — will exist either as pure thought
or something very much like thought:
voltage conditions darting around the Net
at the speed of light, in conditions that one
might behold in effect, as glowing pixels or
transmitted sounds, but never touch or claim
to "own" in the old sense of the word.*

— John Perry Barlow

2.03

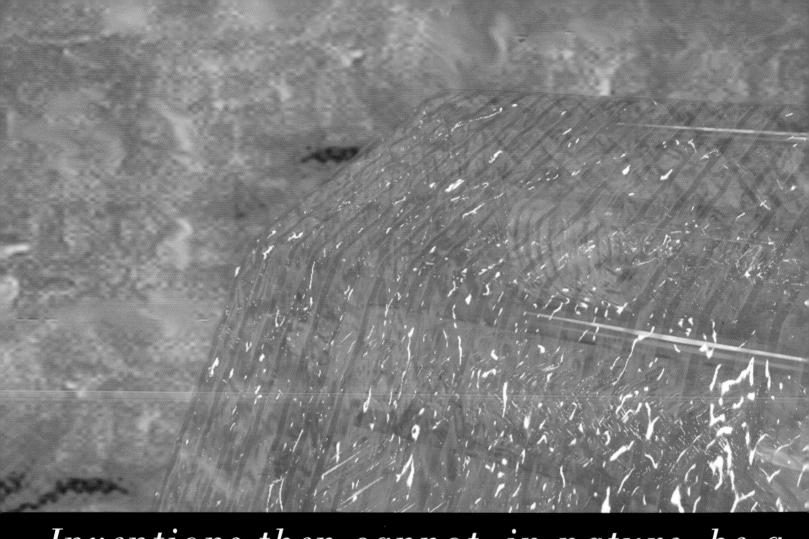

Inventions then cannot, in nature, be a

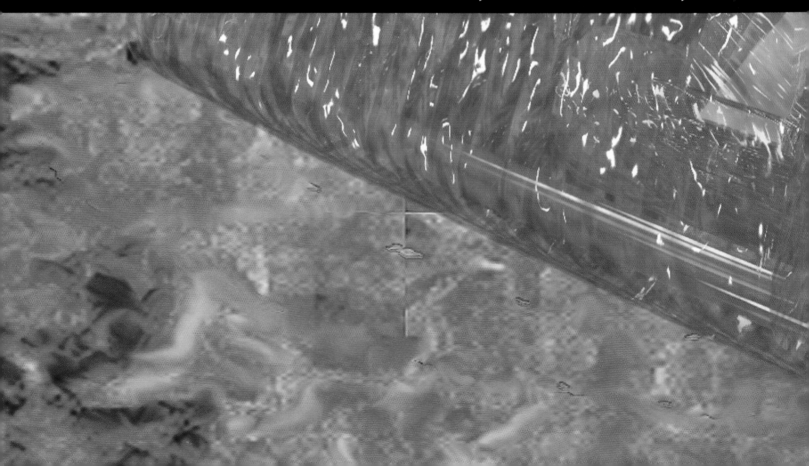

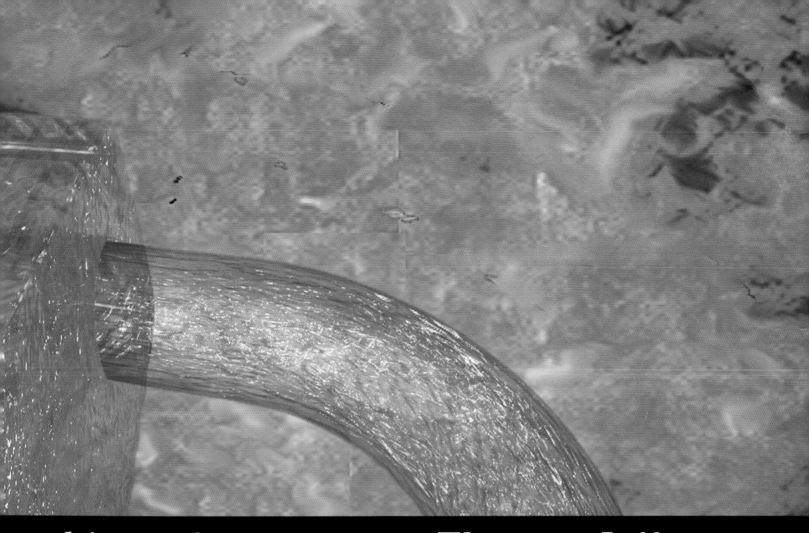
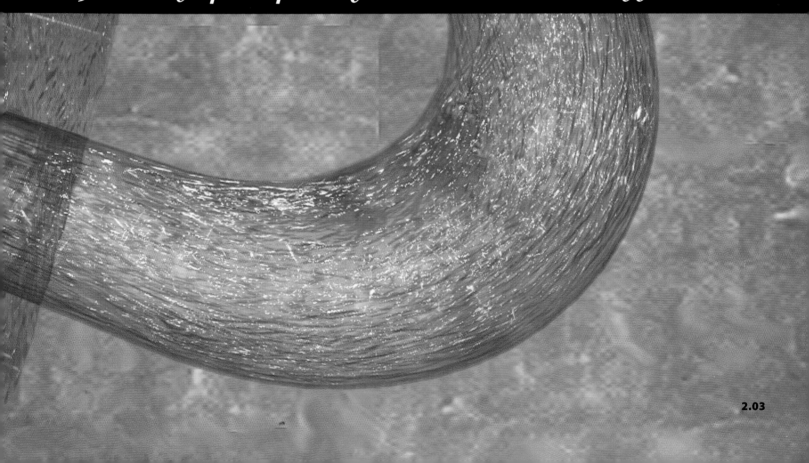

subject of property. – Thomas Jefferson

THE PROTOTYPE

HAS MOVED FROM BEING A THING TO BEING AN IDEA.

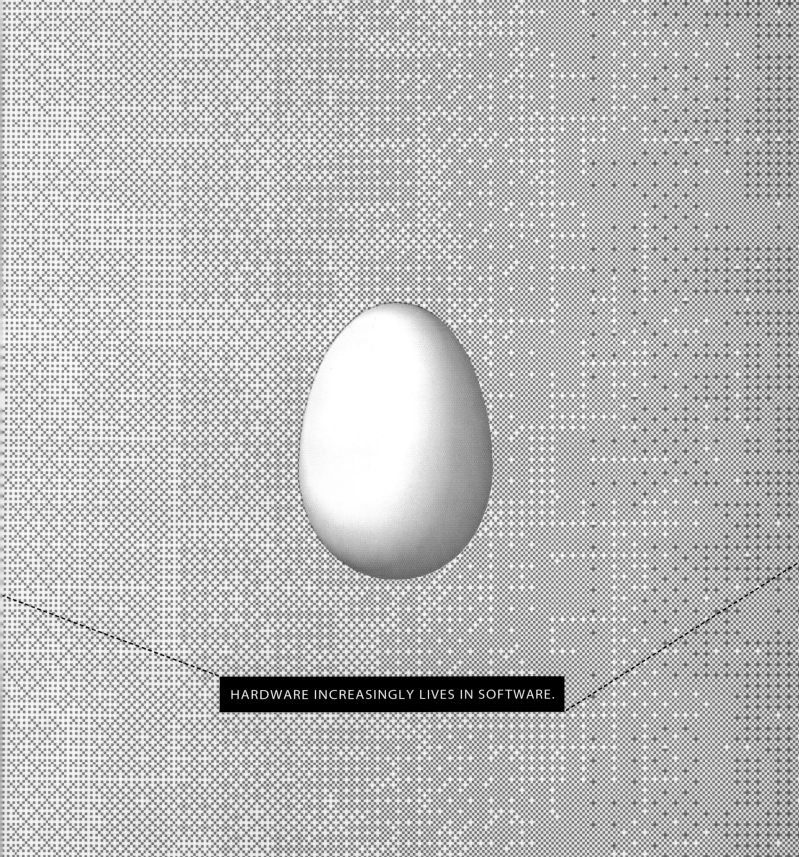

HARDWARE INCREASINGLY LIVES IN SOFTWARE.

TODAY MORE AND MORE PROTOTYPES LIVE INSIDE COMPUTERS.

WHEN IT COMES TO "THE VISION THING," PROTOTYPES HAVE GROWN TO OVERSHADOW FINISHED PRODUCT.

THE CHALLENGE TODAY IS FOR ACTUAL PRODUCTS TO LIVE UP TO THE PROTOTYPES.

PHIL PATTON

*EYE-PROTECTOR FOR CHICKENS. PATENT #730,918 6/16/1903

"There's a new and virulent
cultural

ripping through the world...

virus

strong feelings of

The symptoms of those infected include attacks of **optimism.**

outbreaks of **pronoia**

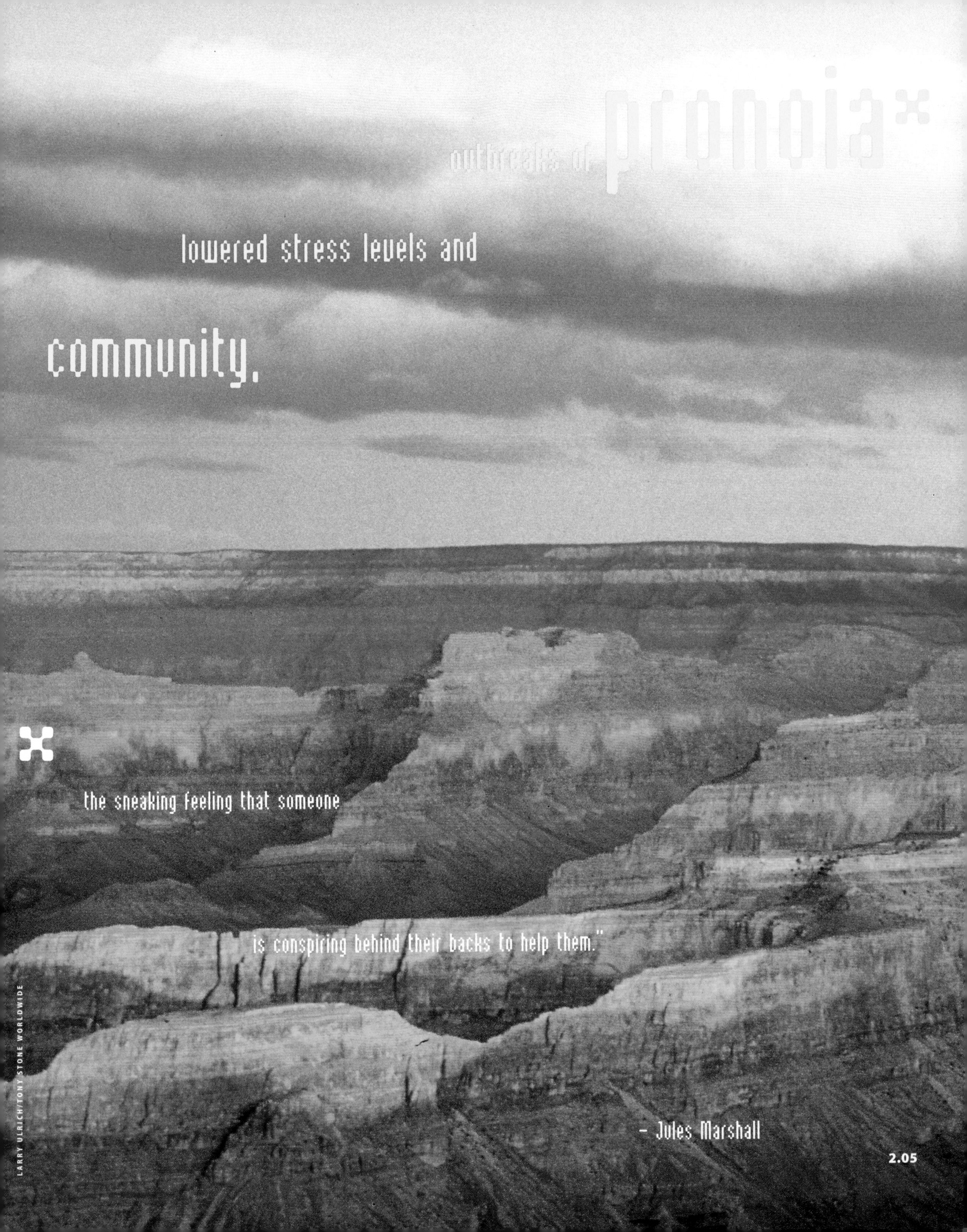

lowered stress levels and

community,

the sneaking feeling that someone

is conspiring behind their backs to help them."

– Jules Marshall

LARRY ULRICH/TONY STONE WORLDWIDE

2.05

"The Net, the very network itself, you

see, is merely a means to an end ....

The end is
to reverse-
engineer
government,

to hack
politics
down to its
component
parts

and fix it."

— Joshua Quittner,

on the Electronic Frontier

Foundation

2.06

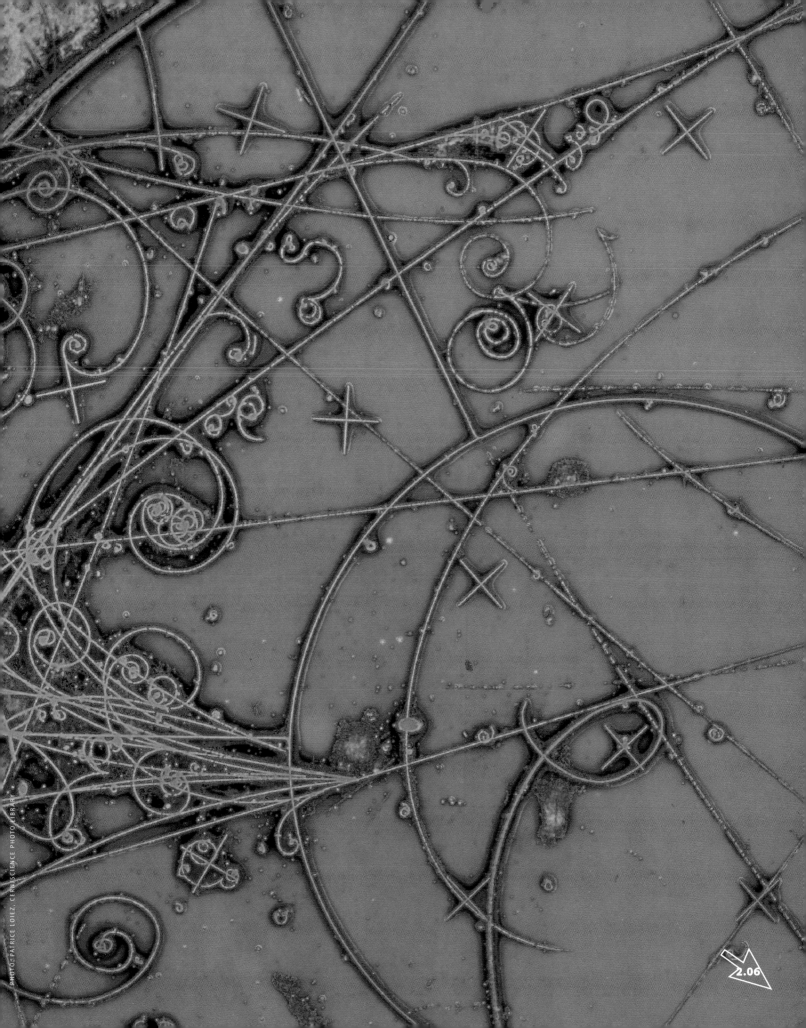

2.06

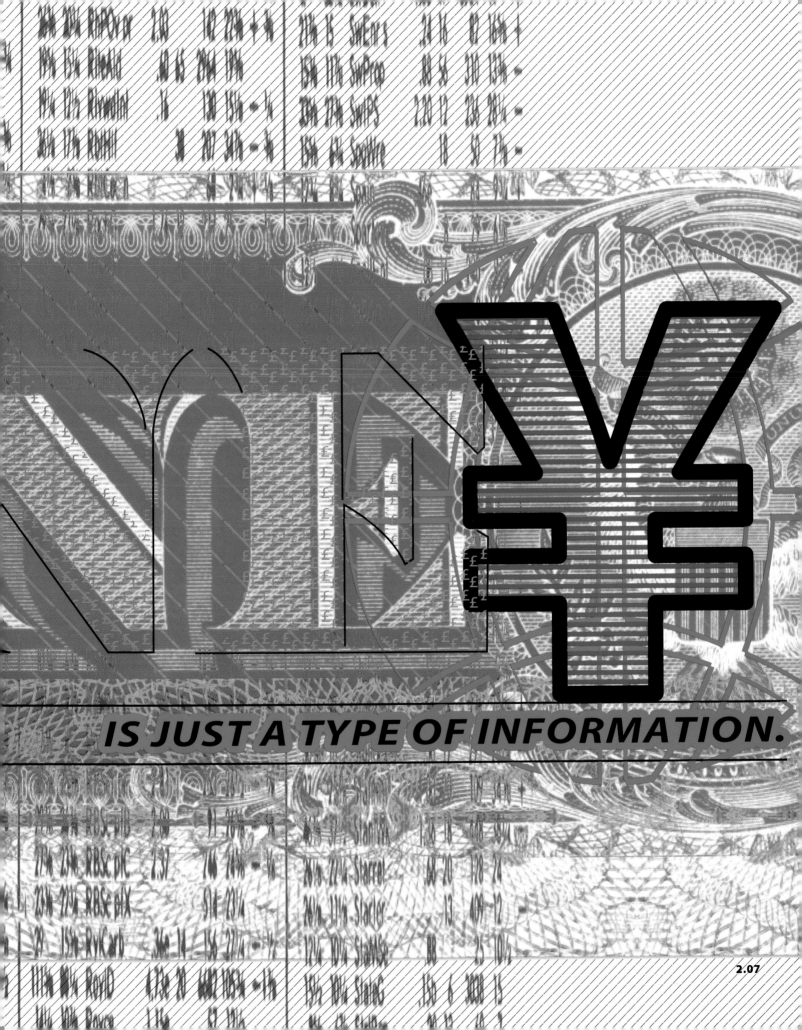

MONEY IS JUST A TYPE OF INFORMATION.

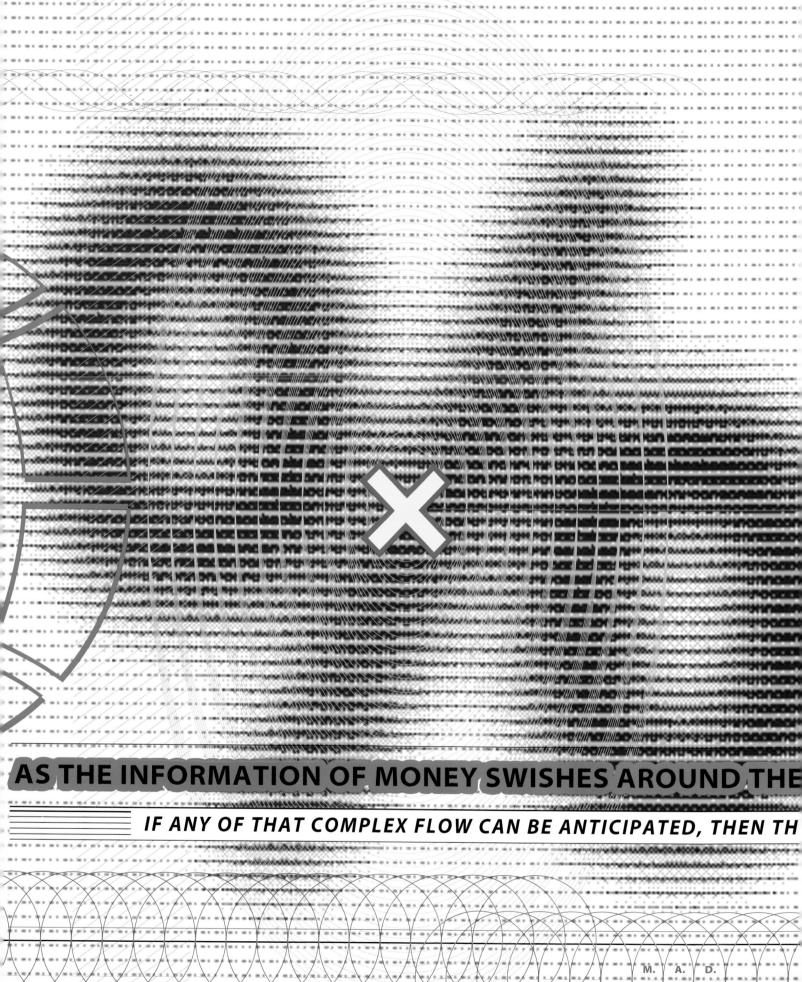

AS THE INFORMATION OF MONEY SWISHES AROUND THE

IF ANY OF THAT COMPLEX FLOW CAN BE ANTICIPATED, THEN TH

M. A. D.

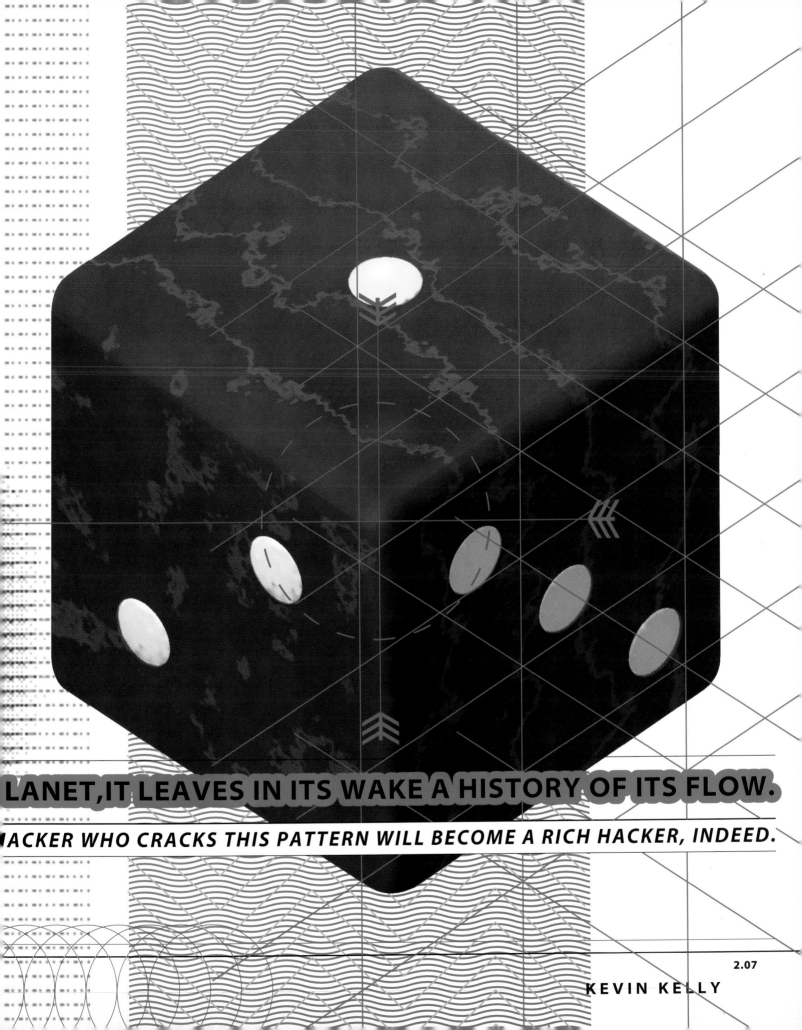

LANET, IT LEAVES IN ITS WAKE A HISTORY OF ITS FLOW.

ACKER WHO CRACKS THIS PATTERN WILL BECOME A RICH HACKER, INDEED.

2.07

KEVIN KELLY

THE ROCK STAR, UP ON STAGE, BATHED IN LIGHT, INACCESSIBLE, IS AN OUTDATED IMAGE FROM A

DEFUNCT

IN A WORLD WHERE INFORMATION PLUS THOSE WHO CONTROL THE EDITING DJs ARE EDITORS OF THE STREET. HUG

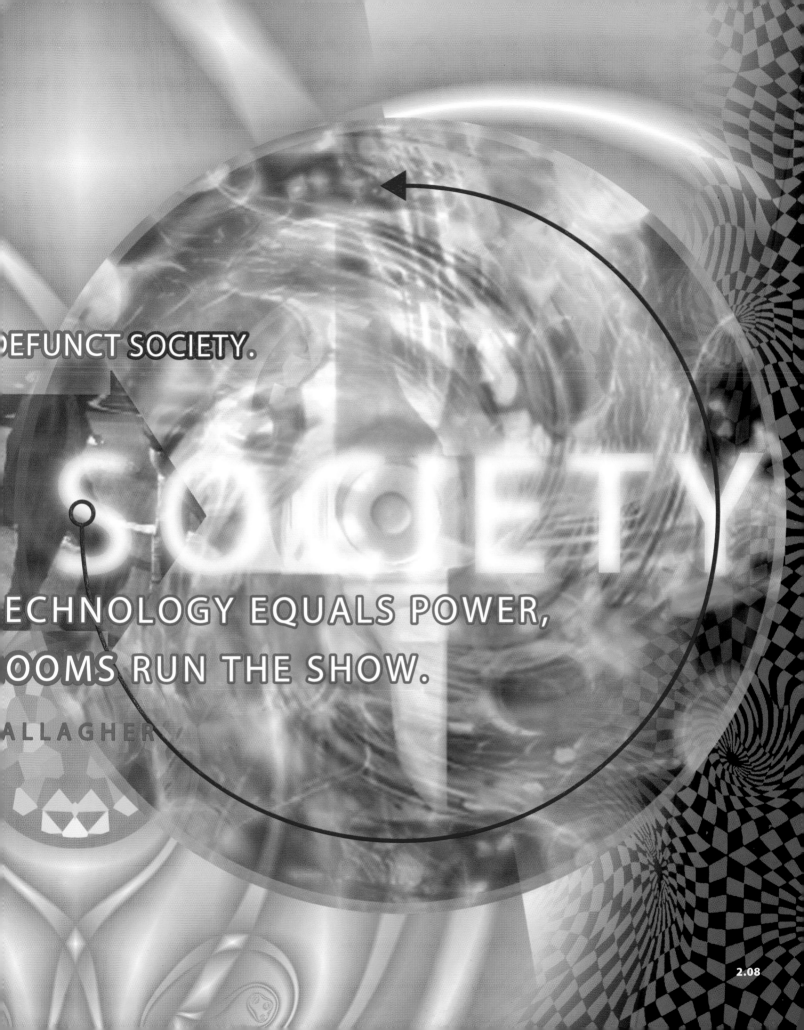

DEFUNCT SOCIETY.

SOCIETY

ECHNOLOGY EQUALS POWER,
OOMS RUN THE SHOW.

ALLAGHER

2.08

...ical exhibitionism, and strategic simulations?

news flash:

2.09

cyber-deterrent

JAMES DER DERIAN

in the 21st century army you get the

2.09

"**NO AMBITION,** HOWEVER EXTRAVAGANT, **NO FANTASY,** HOWEVER OUTLANDISH, CAN ANY LONGER BE DISMISSED AS **CRAZY** OR IMPOSSIBLE. **THIS** IS THE AGE WHEN **YOU** CAN **FINALLY** DO IT ALL...

SUDDENLY TECHNOLOGY HAS GIVEN US POWERS WITH WHICH WE CAN MANIPULATE NOT ONLY EXTERNAL REALITY— THE PHYSICAL WORLD – BUT ALSO, AND MUCH MORE PORTENTOUSLY, OURSELVES.

YOU CAN BECOME **WHATEVER** YOU WANT TO BE." – ED REGIS, ON EXTROPIANS

2.10

2.10

USA CCCP UNESCO NA

AFL-CIO FDA FCC NY

DOJ INTERPOL DOE D

SDS OAS AMA DARPA G

MITI GE NASA NSF

CBS NBC COMMODORE

MCI GO RCA INTEL A

NPR EMI IBM IRS AP

MOTOROLA FORD DEC

PAN AM EASTERN PTL

HONDA PTA NEA TOYO

ASCAP MIT MASONS BP

The only stability is in accepting

GY NAACP NAFTA BM
E FBI NEXT DOT IRA
D AARP NRA EDR PLO
R CIA BELL DNA ARPA
H CDL WHO ABC AT&T
NN TCI FOX PBS MIT
C INTERNET BC GBN
LE SUN SINGER UNIX
IRCHILD APOLLO BMW
GM NASDAQ CHRYSLER
A HP FEDEX UPS SAT
E LDS IOOC AIGA NEA
NHL AMEX BCCI FO

ABILITY

2.11

Luther Diller Gorb

Demming Ford Spock

uling Sarnoff Turi

u Bann ster

ch Robinson Zapat

ld lu a Esch

er Thoreau Buddha

on Emerson Sar

Organizations have to be systematically open to

rconi Burr Pelagiu

no Bell Mohammed M

Christ Wycliffe

kHeisenberg Moo

obs Iacocca Socra
chev Edison Hearst
Rushdie Owens Sadat
g Ferrari Montesso
Ftler Murdoch Slo
Da Vinci Turner Wat
ne Einstein M lo
asso Lincoln McL
ge c e
Bloch Pollock Gand
pplethorp Marx Dar
lsberg Kepler Enge
iss Koresh Von Neu

ESW

– Pierre A. Wack

"A generation ago, almost everyone shared common

media.

That universality has been shattered, probably for good.
Information now splits along demographic, political and cultural fault lines...

…We all look into our separate mirrors now, and mostly see **ourselves** looking back.

What was universal in the post-war years has become the media of the middle class, the political and policy structure,

he aging and increasingly **self-righteous** boomers." — Jon Katz

Ralph Steiner

Power Switches, circa 1930

Hans Bellmer

The Doll, 1934-35

MACHINES WILL NEVER BE ABLE TO GIVE THE THINKING PROCESS A MODEL OF THOUGHT ITSELF, SINCE MACHINES ARE NOT MORTAL.

3.01

WHAT GIVES HUMANS ACCESS TO THE SYMBOLIC DOMAIN OF VALUE AND MEANING IS THE FACT THAT WE DIE.

James Porto ▶
Centuries End, 1994

– *Régis Debray*

Every virus turned out into the computer wilds is also a carrier for the purest and strongest signal a human being can send.

"Remember my name," the virus says, which after all is just another way of saying, "I'm alive."

-Julian Dibbell

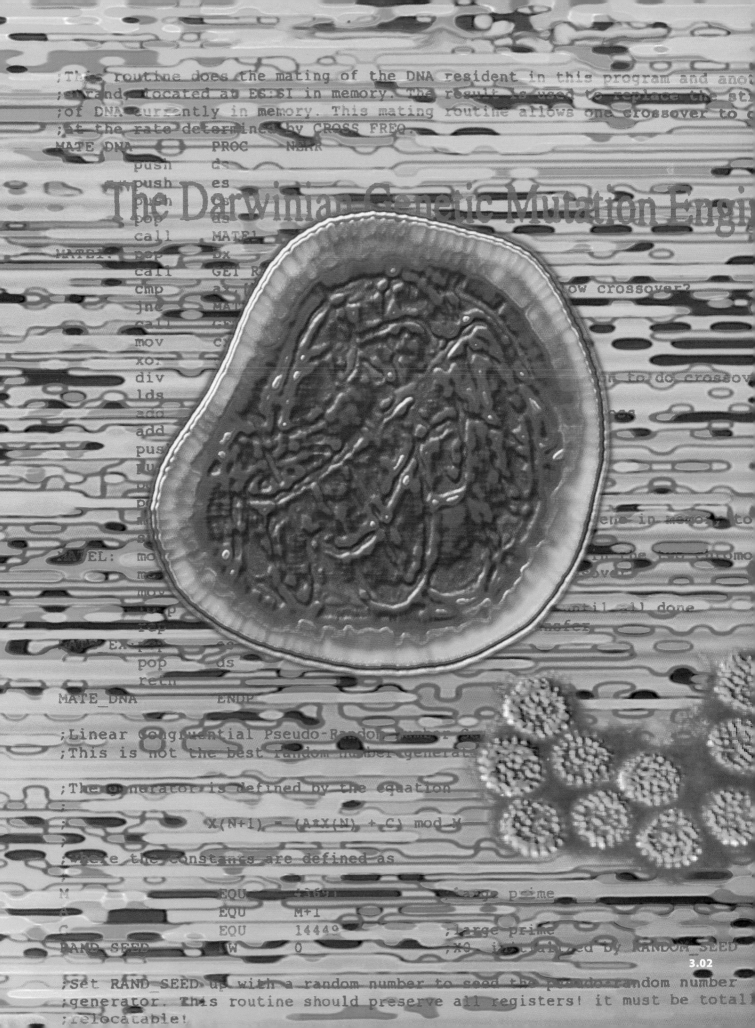

```
;This routine does the mating of the DNA resident in this program and anot
;strand located at ES:SI in memory. The result is used to replace the str
;of DNA currently in memory. This mating routine allows one crossover to o
;at the rate determined by CROSS_FREQ.
MATE_DNA        PROC    NEAR
                push    ds
                push    es
                pop     ds
                call    MATE1
MATE1:          pop     bx
                call    GET_R
                cmp     a                           ow crossover?
                jne     MAT
                call
                mov     c
                xo
                div                                   to do crossov
                lds
                add
                add
                pus
                lo
                p
                m                                     ene in memory
                p
MATEL:          mo                                          he 1st chromo
                mo                                           over
                mov
                loop                                        until all done
                rep
MATE_EX                                                fer
                pop     ds
                ret
MATE_DNA        ENDP

;Linear Congruential Pseudo-Random number
;This is not the best random number generat

;The generator is defined by the equation
;
;       X(N+1) = (A*X(N) + C) mod M
;
;where the constants are defined as
;
M               EQU     28421                         ;large prime
                EQU     M+1
C               EQU     14449                         ;large prime
RAND_SEED       DW      0                             ;X0 initialized by RANDOM_SEED
```

3.02

```
;Set RAND_SEED up with a random number to seed the pseudorandom number
;generator. This routine should preserve all registers! it must be total
;relocatable!
```

Even with the explosion from the grass there's still going to be a need for mass culture,

roots,

4 5 6 7 8

for truly great

links

people together.

— Scott Sassa

entertainment that transcends

.all the little

niches

and

The struggle
to control culture

is eternal.

with one ethical value system fighting to supplant another,

Elvis presided over the birth of a great new means of expression,

The second was television

one of three such flowerings in America since World War II.

from broadcast to cable to music videos.

The proBleM wIth cOMPutErS iS thAt th

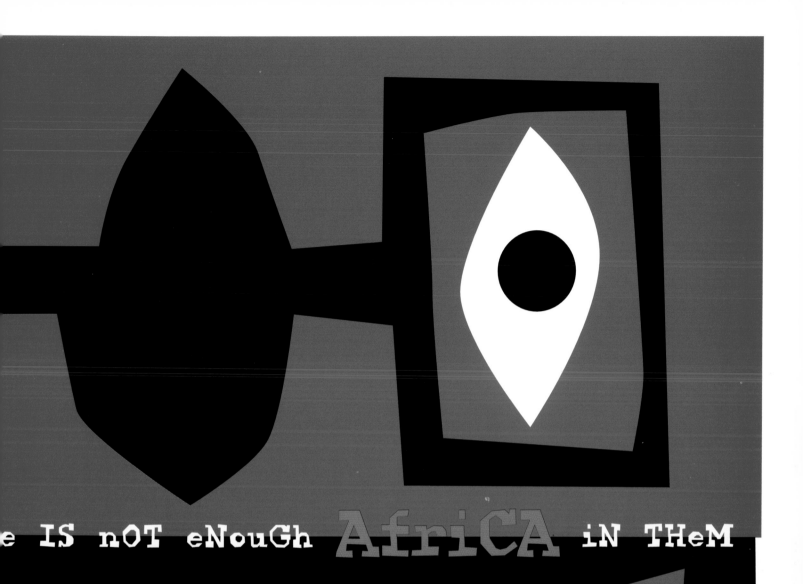

e IS nOT eNouGh AfriCA iN THeM

WHaT's PIsSing ME oFf iS thAt ThEY usE so liTtlE oF m

BODY

brIAn eNO

3.05

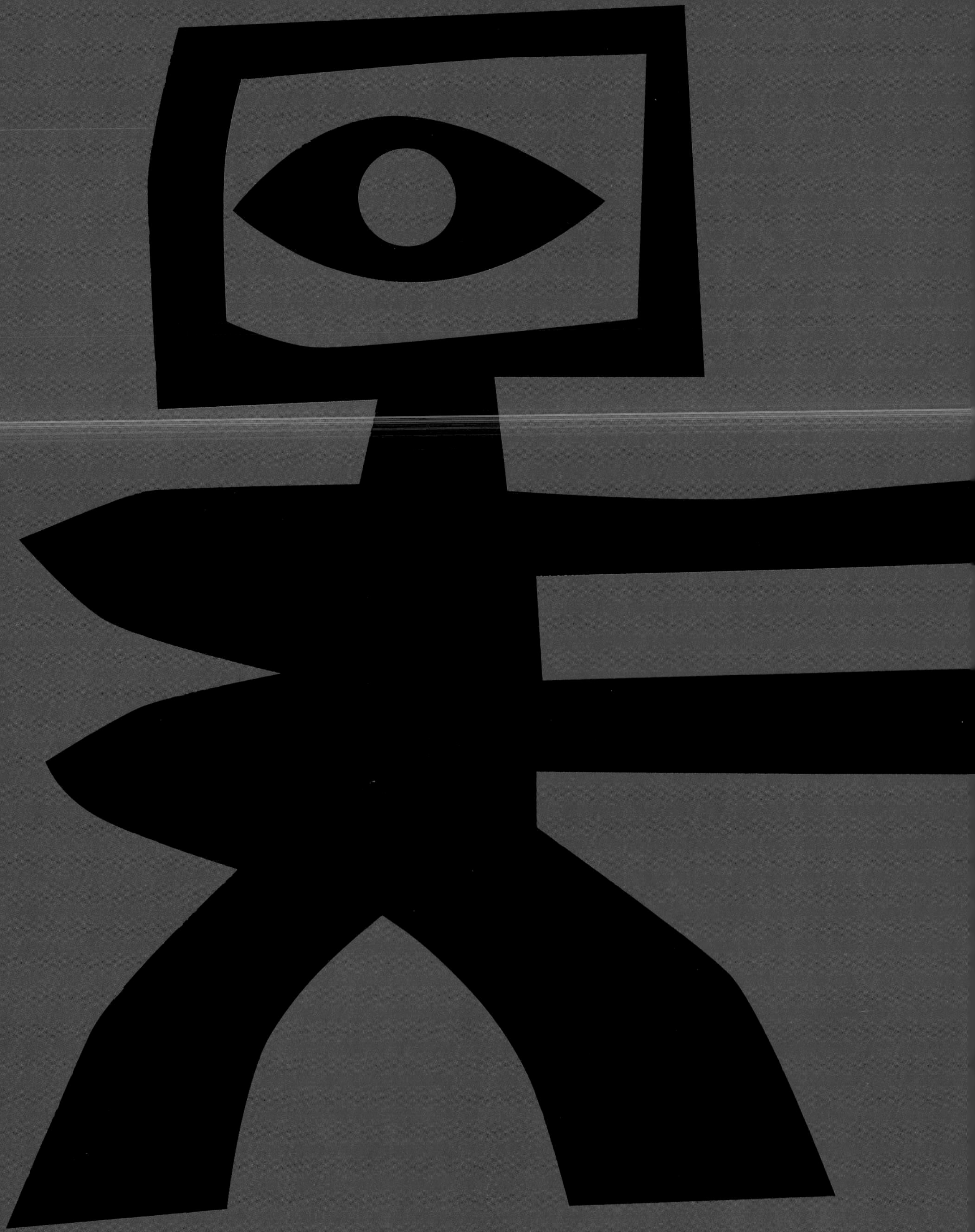

THINKING

THE TASK OF   IS BASED

REMEMBERING

E T V E

T V H

IS WEIRDLY

SELECTION UPON AND WEEDING OUT; TRYING IRNYG SIMILAR TO FORGETTING EVERYTHING.

MOST THINGS THAT PEOPLE DO SHOULDN'T BE REMEMBERED.

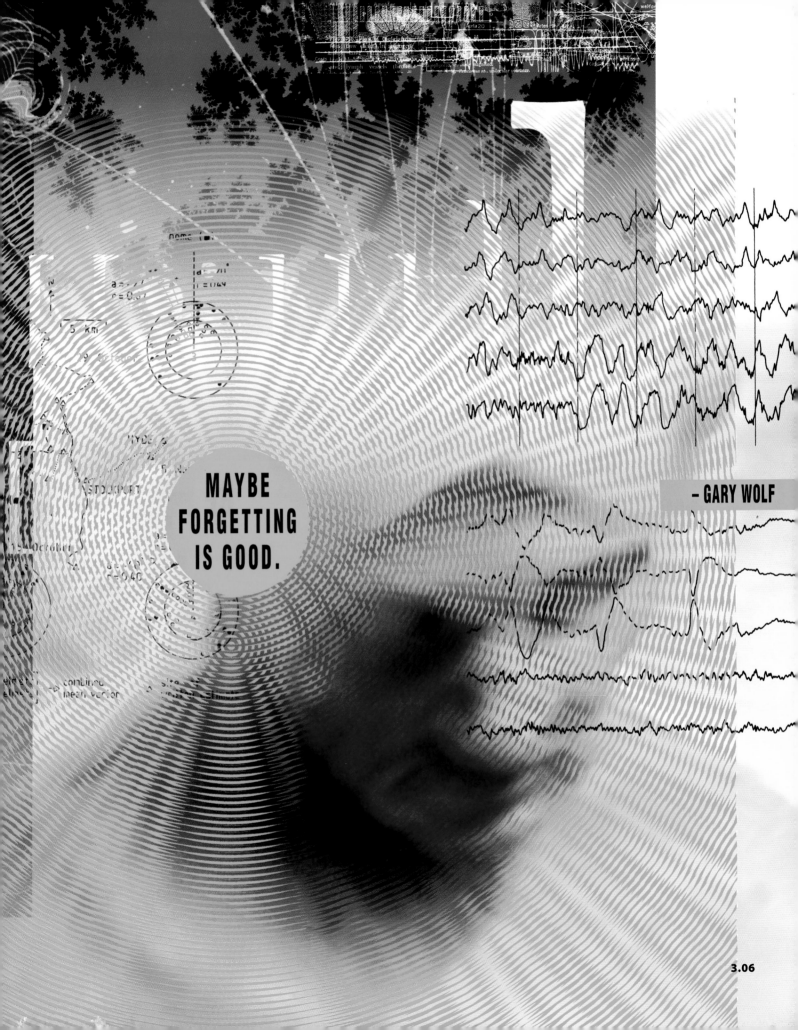

MAYBE
FORGETTING
IS GOOD.

– GARY WOLF

Not only

does the body of an organism   march to the orders of   its genes,

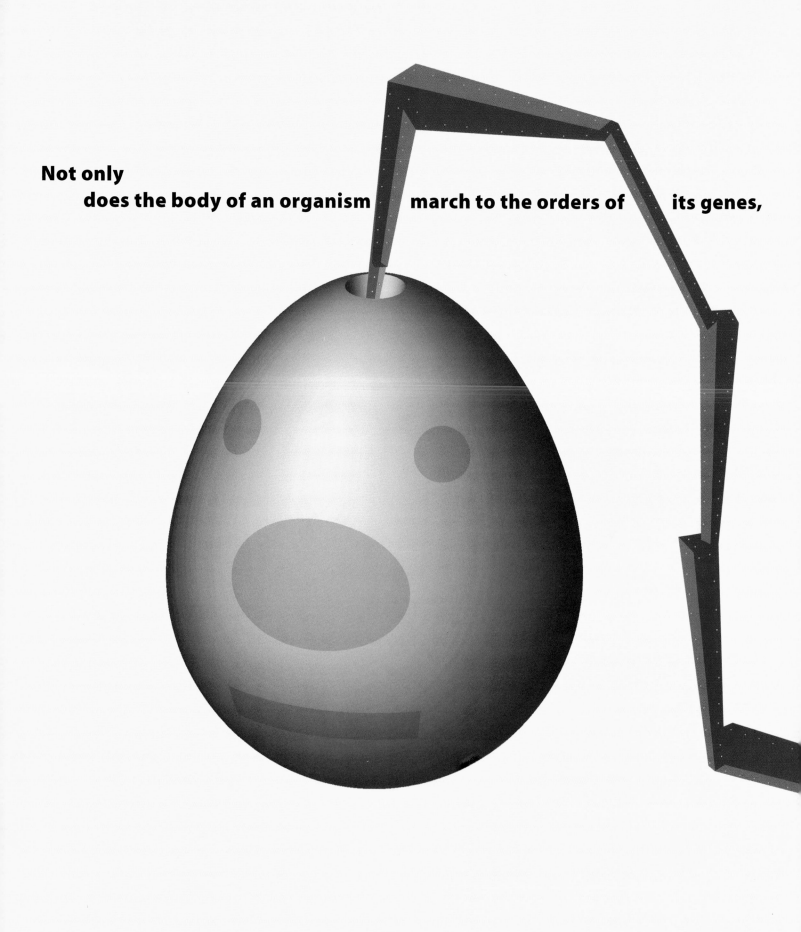

but so do the artifacts the organism builds or uses.

(In this sense,
the egg uses both a
chicken and a nest to
make another egg,
and so the nest, too,
is an evolutionary
extension of the egg.)

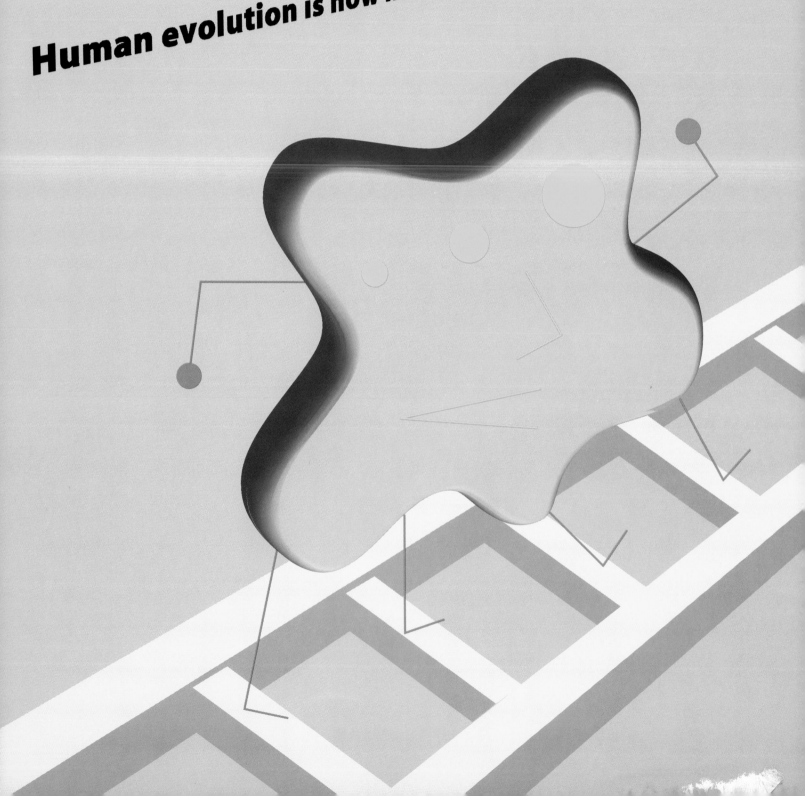

Human evolution is now inextricably bound up with technological evolution.

Humankind is co-evolving with its artifacts, and the genes that can't cope with that new reality will not survive into future millennia.

– Michael Schrage

3.07

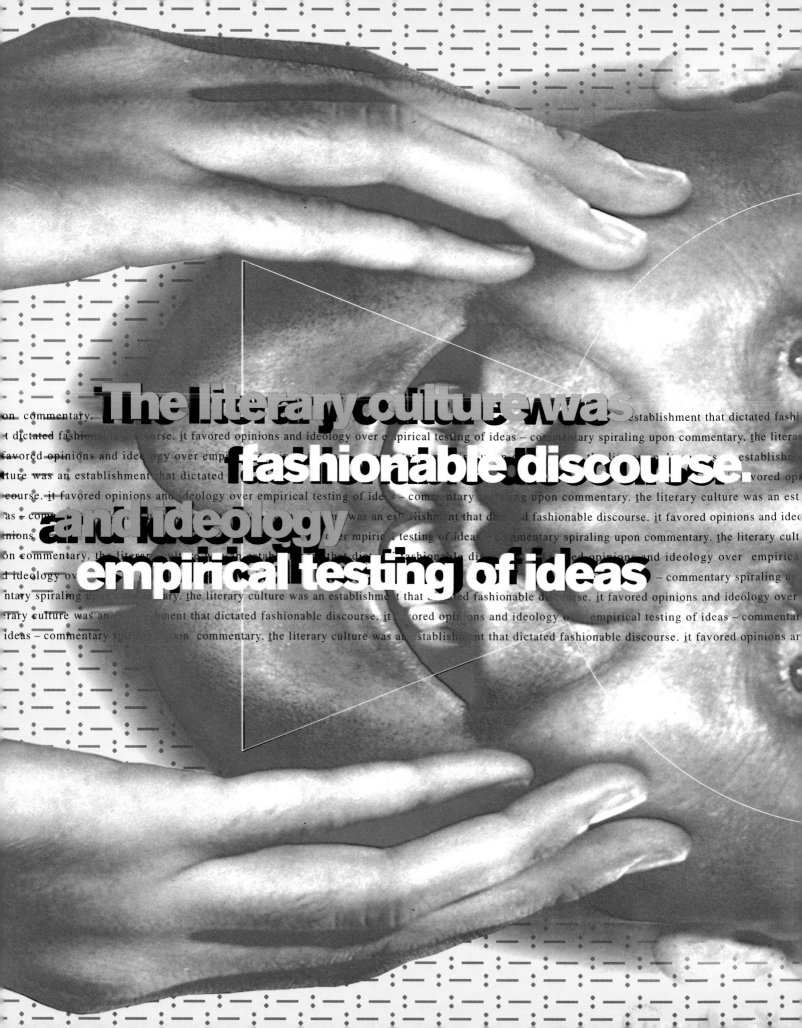

The literary culture was fashionable discourse. and ideology empirical testing of ideas

on commentary. the literary culture was establishment that dictated fashi t dictated fashionable discourse. it favored opinions and ideology over empirical testing of ideas – commentary spiraling upon commentary. the litera favored opinions and ideology over empir fashionable discourse it favored opinions ss establish ture was an establishment that dictated fashionable discourse it favored op course. it favored opinions and ideology over empirical testing of ideas – commentary spiraling upon commentary. the literary culture was an est as comp was an establishment that dictated fashionable discourse. it favored opinions and ideo nions er mpiric testing of ideas commentary spiraling upon commentary. the literary cult on commentary. the literary culture was an establ that di fashionable dis ed opinions and ideology over empirica d ideology ov mpiric testing of ideas – commentary spiraling u ntary spiraling u ary. the literary culture was an establishme t that dicted fashionable di course. it favored opinions and ideology over rary culture was an blishment that dictated fashionable discourse. it vored opinions and ideology o empirical testing of ideas – commentar ideas – commentary spir upon commentary. the literary culture was an establishment that dictated fashionable discourse. it favored opinions an

an establishment that dictated it favored opinions over —commentary spiraling upon commentary.

A(ttitude?

(<u>as</u> as a cultural force

m.A.D.

it's a dead end.

— John Brockman

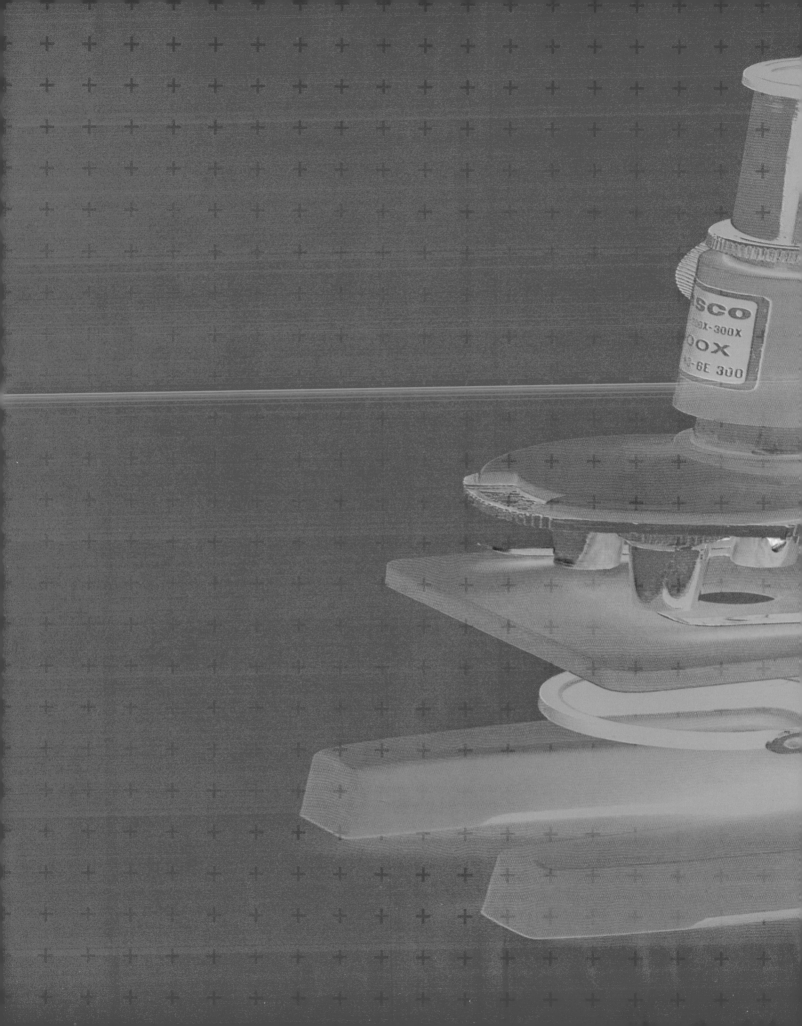

"Our communal and civic open spaces – courts, workplaces, Con are no longe

gress, Academe, the media —

places where issues are settled ...

2.09

... but **battlegrounds** on which our most pressing

conflicts will never be resolved."
— Jon Katz

3.09

Today,

people

who retire

created

by industry.

As industry

more

wealth,

allowing

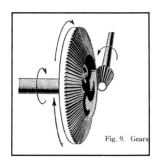

are supported ———→

via wealth ———→

that is ultimately

becomes more ———→

efficient, ———→

there will be

people ———→

to retire ———→

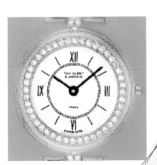

earlier. ———→

When industry is totally automated and hyper-efficient, it will create so much wealth that retirement can begin at birth. - Hans Moravec

3.10

"Two styles of people: guys and gals.
Females, what? They caretake. They nurture.
Men, what? They squirt and move on.

So, business start-ups

3.11

Venture capitalists, though?

Gigolos. Roosters. Seed capital. Get it?"

— Po Bronson

"WHAT THE NET IS, MORE THAN ANYTHING ELSE AT THIS POINT, IS A PLATFORM FOR

ENTREPRENEURIAL ACTIVITIES — A FREE-MARKET ECONOMY IN ITS TRUEST SENSE ...

3.12

... IT'S A LEVEL PLAYING FIELD WHERE PEOPLE CAN DO ANYTHING THEY WANT TO."

– MARC ANDREESSEN

COLD AND SWEET

3.12

3.12

END

The following pages provide mental and hyper links to each mind grenade:

First, we describe the creative process (design); then there's a short bio of the person from whom the quote came (quote); next, are credits for the artists and photographers (imagery); and finally, a URL that takes you to the complete *Wired* story from which the quote was taken (story).

John Plunkett
Creative Director, *Wired*
San Francisco

1.01

Design: We thought it was only fitting that the introduction to *Wired*'s premiere issue begin with a 25-year-old quote from our patron saint, Marshall McLuhan. The statement is actually the first paragraph of McLuhan's only bestseller, *The Medium Is the Massage.*
Quentin Fiore's 1967 design for this book combined word and image in a way that transformed our notions of what a book should be, and was a real touchstone in our development of the introductions in *Wired.*
Each month, we try to focus readers' attention on the most important or provocative idea in that issue. McLuhan's statement is really the subtext of every *Wired* issue. The visual metaphors are meant to amplify the message–that individual's lives are being transformed and connected on a global scale, via and because of new technology. The nonlinear typography is likewise intended to signal that our means of sending and receiving text messages is moving from the print realm to electronic media.
This was also the first of many collaborations with the talented illustrator/designer Erik Adigard.
Quote: Marshall McLuhan, *Wired*'s patron saint and media prophet.
Imagery: Erik Adigard/MAD

1.02

Design: For our second issue we returned to McLuhan (we do this in every issue, by including a tiny quote of his that appears embedded in the masthead). We chose stock news photos of current events (as well as our own photo of Willard the Weatherman) to illustrate the collision and frequent collapse of old cultures as they encounter new technologies. William Gibson fans may recognize that the background imagery used here derives from the first line of his book *Neuromancer:* "The sky was the color of television."
Quote: Marshall McLuhan, *Wired*'s patron saint and media prophet.
Imagery: India: Jeff Greenwald; neo-Nazis: Sacha Hartgers/ Matrix; Madonna: Marc Morrison/Shooting Star; Iraqi women: Gregory Heisler/The Image Bank; Yeltsin: Klaus Reisinger/Black Star; George Bush: Gerald Shumann/Picture Group; Josh Pearson of EBN, taken from the enhanced CD Telecommunication Breakdown (TVT Records)

1.03

Design: To illustrate Mitch Kapor's contention that cyberspace better serves individuals and communities than mass audiences, we contrasted an image of Telluride, Colorado (one of the first communities to install its own Web node with community access) with abstract realizations of cyberspace, and finished the sequence with the image of a lone but very wired individual.
Quote: Mitchell Kapor, creator of Lotus 1-2-3 and co-founder of the Electronic Frontier Foundation, an advocacy group for cyber rights.
Imagery: backgrounds: Scott Clum; mountains: Ken Gallard/Telluride Company; Switchboard: Herbert/Archive; Winking: A. E. Finch/Archive; man at sink: Richard Haffar/ Curtis Pearson/1996 © Curtis Pearson Studios
Story:
http://www.hotwired.com/wired/ 1.3/features/kapor.on.nii.html

1.04

Design: Erik Adigard's visualization of Michael Crichton's media dinosaur took the form of a Big-mass-media-Mac, followed by an explosion of today's opiate of the masses. The exploding vehicle shown is based on a sequence NBC news ran, which purported to show the possibility of the fuel tank in a certain model of GM truck exploding when the vehicle was sideswiped. NBC later admitted that the sequence had been staged.

Quote: Michael Crichton, the best-selling author of *The Andromeda Strain, Jurassic Park, Rising Sun,* and *Disclosure.*

Imagery: Erik Adigard/MAD

Story:

http://www.hotwired.com/wired/ 1.4/features/mediasaurus.html

1.05

Design: Nick Philip pushed Photoshop and the collaging of found imagery to the edge to illustrate Alvin Toffler's observation of the transition from mass to micro (and multiple) new phenomena.

Quote: Alvin Toffler, a futurist and the best-selling author of *Future Shock, The Third Wave,* and *War and Anti-War.*

Imagery: Nick Philip/H20 Media

Story:

http://www.hotwired.com/wired/ 1.5/features/toffler.html

1.06

Design: Fred Davis utilized subtle layering techniques (including a matte tinted varnish) to visualize Brenda Laurel's thoughts on immersive versus transmitted media experiences. *Wired* designer Thomas Schneider completed the experience with a cool dip in a blue pool.

Quote: Brenda Laurel, a researcher at Interval Research Corp. in Palo Alto, where she focuses on human-computer interaction and cultural aspects of technology; editor of

the book *The Art of Human-Computer Design;* and author of *Computers as Theatre.*

Imagery: intro: Fred Davis; reflections on water: Yukimasa Hirota/Photonica

Story:

http://www.hotwired.com/wired/ 1.6/features/wired.wonders.html

2.01

Design: Stock imagery of everyone's worst surgery nightmare was contrasted with a child playing (and amplified with metallic inks and Adobe Photoshop filters) to symbolize the coming shift in health care reported by Joe Flower–from last-minute traumatic procedures to as-early-as-possible applications of information. Erik Adigard altered the stock photos.

Quote: Joe Flower, the author of *Prince of the Magic Kingdom: Michael Eisner and the Making of Disney.*

Imagery: intro: Erik Adigard/MAD; surgery: Kay Chemush/Image Bank; girl in grass: Jiro Fukagawa/ Photonica

Story:

http://www.hotwired.com/wired/ 2.01/features/healthcare.html

2.02

Design: For our special issue on the future of advertising, Erik Adigard created a happy inter-face between sender and receiver. We followed it with a sales pitch on

the kind of soap *Wired* sells– content.

Quote: Michael Schrage, a Media Lab Fellow, and author of *No More Teams!: The Dynamics of Creative Collaboration.*

Imagery: intro: Erik Adigard/MAD; icons: Jim Ludtke

Story:

http://www.hotwired.com/wired/ 2.02/features/advertising.html

2.03

Design: To emphasize quotes from Thomas Jefferson and John Perry Barlow that focused on the difficulty of "owning" an idea, we carved Barlow's statement in stone (via Adobe Photoshop), ran Jefferson's across a virtual lock, and finished with copper handcuffs built from the copyright symbol.

Quote: John Perry Barlow, Republican Deadhead and co-founder and executive chair of the Electronic Frontier Foundation, an advocacy group for cyber rights. Thomas Jefferson was third president of the United States.

Imagery: intro: Erik Adigard/MAD; lock renderings: courtesy of Autodesk, Inc.

Story:

http://www.hotwired.com/wired/ 2.03/features/economy.ideas.html

2.04

Design: Erik Adigard found a new twist on the chicken-or-the-egg riddle to help make Phil Patton's point about the growing importance of design prototypes; Erik even went so far as to find a genuine patent, from 1903, for an eye-protector for chickens.

Quote: Phil Patton, a contributing editor to *Esquire* and regular contributor to *Wired.*

Imagery: Erik Adigard/MAD

Story:

http://www.hotwired.com/wired/
2.04/features/dreamware.html

2.05

Design: For a story on Zippies—an unlikely fusion of the UK dance scene, cyber street tech, and paganism—we presented the musicians Tambours du Bronx and an image from a transcendental software program.

Quote: Jules Marshall, the editor of *Mediamatic*, an Amsterdam-based techno-culture magazine.

Imagery: Grand Canyon: Larry Ulrich/Tony Stone; Zippies and the Tambours du Bronx: Floris Leeuwenberg/TCS; orb: HEX; font: Union Round, a [T-26] release

Story:

http://www.hotwired.com/wired/
2.05/features/zippies.html

2.06

Design: We juxtaposed stock images of Washington's major monuments to convey a key aspect of the Electronic Frontier Foundations philosophy–that the Net could be a means to "reverse-engineer" government.

Quote: Joshua Quittner, technology reporter for *Time* and editor of Netley News, a news website.

Imagery: starry sky: Westlight; Jefferson Memorial and Lincoln Memorial: Larry Lee/Westlight; clouds background: Doug Armand/Tony Stone Images; Capitol: Dale E. Boyer/Photo Researchers; Washington Monument: Chris Cheadle/Tony Stone Images; particle tracks: Photo Researchers

Story:

http://www.hotwired.com/wired/
2.06/features/eff.html

2.07

Design: We overlaid symbols of the Deutsche Mark, the Japanese yen, and the British pound onto an American dollar bill to spell M-O-N-E-Y, followed on the next spread by a die and percentages, to mirror Kevin Kelly's thoughts on the hacking of information flows in the currency and stock markets.

Quote: Kevin Kelly, executive editor at *Wired* and author of *Out of Control: The Rise of Neo-Biological Civilization.*

Imagery: Erik Adigard/MAD

Story:

http://www.hotwired.com/wired/
2.07/features/wall.st.html

2.08

Design: Hugh Gallagher's thoughts about the ascendance of the DJ in the music world inspired us to run a rock star (Eddie Vedder of Pearl Jam) through the cultural blender.

Quote: Hugh Gallagher, a freelance writer based in New York.

Imagery: intro: Erik Adigard/MAD; Eddie Vedder: Mark Morrison/Shooting Star

Story:

http://www.hotwired.com/wired/
2.08/features/spooky.html

2.09

Design: Screen-grabs from the Gulf War, including a blow-up of CNN's miniseries-like logo, helped make James Der Derian's point that the new military-deterrence model may be information- and demo-based.

Quote: James Der Derian, the author of *Antidiplomacy: Spies, Terror, Speed, and War* and *Virtual Security.*

Imagery: intro: Erik Adigard/MAD; CNN Gulf War: Jacques Witt/Sipa Press

Story:

http://www.hotwired.com/wired/
2.09/features/cyber.deter.html

2.10

Design: James Porto's surreal imagery brought life to the Extropians belief that we can all transform ourselves (literally) via technology.

Quote: Ed Regis, the author of *Great Mambo Chicken and the Transhuman Condition: Science Slightly Over the Edge.*

Imagery: intro: James Porto; running man: Mars Safrogelev; photo of barb-wired head: Jeff Rigby; sculpture of barb-wired head: Scott Silken

Story:

http://www.hotwired.com/wired/
2.10/features/extropians.html

2.11

Design: Pierre A. Wack, the creator of modern scenario planning, makes the somewhat heretical point that organizations, in order to really survive, must be open to both uncertainty and hearsay. To help make the point we contrasted the acronyms of large (and many now defunct) organizations with a sort of honor roll of famous heretical thinkers.

Quote: Pierre A. Wack, head of business environment research for Shell Group Planning in the 1970s, helped pioneer "scenario planning."

Imagery: intro: John Plunkett/ Thomas Schneider. Typography by Thomas Schneider.

Story:

http://www.hotwired.com/wired/
2.11/features/gbn.html

2.12

Design: Anchorman Walter Cronkite and a baby-boomer with a media-monkey on his back helped frame Jon Katz's comments on the fragmentation of media.

Quote: Jon Katz, a media critic and former executive producer of the CBS Evening News.

Imagery: intro: Erik Adigard/ Patricia McShane/MAD; Edward Murrow: UPI/Corbis/ Bettmann

Story:

http://www.hotwired.com/wired/ 2.12/departments/electro sphere/killjoy.html

3.01

Design: For our anniversary issue we printed in black & white. Classic "machine-age" photos from the 1930s by Abbott, Bellmer, and Steiner were contrasted with James Porto's digital collage of a fallen angel, to amplify Régis Debray's thoughts on machines and man, thinking, and mortality.

Quote: Régis Debray, who fought beside Che Guevara in Bolivia in the 1960s, and was jailed for his actions; today, his obsession isn't ideology–it's "mediology."

Imagery: Power Switches: Ralph Steiner/The Metropolitan Museum of Art, Ford Motor Company Collection, Gift of the Ford Motor Company and John

C. Waddell, 1987/1987.1100.277; Nightview: Berenice Abbott/ Commerce Graphics Ltd., Inc.; Centuries End, 1994: James Porto, Model: Kimber Bogard; The Doll: Hans Bellmer/The Metropolitan Museum of Art, Ford Motor Company Collection, Gift of the Ford Motor Company and John C. Waddell, 1987/1987.1100.15

Story:

http://www.hotwired.com/wired/ 3.01/features/debray.html

3.02

Design: Johan Vipper created scarily viral pages for this statement about computer viruses.

Quote: Julian Dibbell, a staff writer at *Time* and a contributor to the *Village Voice*.

Imagery: intro: Johan Vipper/MTV; viruses: Photo Researchers

Story:

http://www.hotwired.com/wired/ 3.02/features/viruses.html

3.03

Design: Mass culture and grass-roots were the two sides of the coin in Scott Sassa's statement that Fred Davis responded to visually.

Quote: Scott Sassa, president of Turner Entertainment Group, a division of Turner Broadcasting.

Imagery: Fred Davis

Story:

http://www.hotwired.com/wired/ 3.03/features/sassa.html

3.04

Design: Erik Adigard adapted cultural symbols from Elvis to the Statue of Liberty's torch to help make Jon Katz's point about culture's transition, from television broadcast to cable to the Net.

Quote: Jon Katz, a media critic and former executive producer of the CBS Evening News.

Imagery: Erik Adigard/MAD

Story:

http://www.hotwired.com/wired/ 3.04/departments/electro sphere/elvis.html

3.05

Design: Max Kisman's hand-made imagery married well with Brian Eno's frustrations over the coolness of computers.

Quote: Brian Eno, who is considered the father of ambient music and is a visiting professor at the Royal College of Art in London.

Imagery: Max Kisman

Story:

http://www.hotwired.com/wired/ 3.05/features/eno.html

3.06

Design: Writer Gary Wolf's thoughts about the complexity of memory led us to the complex and evocative imagery of Jeff Brice.

Quote: Gary Wolf, executive editor of HotWired, and co-author (with Michael Stein) of *Aether Madness: An Offbeat Guide to the Online World*.

Imagery: Jeff Brice

Story:

http://www.hotwired.com/wired/ 3.06/features/xanadu.html

3.07

Design: John Hersey's 3-D cartoons allowed us to visualize Michael Schrage's report on the ideas of Richard Dawkin's–that human evolution is now inextricably bound up with technical evolution.

Quote: Michael Schrage, a Media Lab Fellow, and author of *No More Teams!: The Dynamics of Creative Collaboration*.

Imagery: John Hersey

Story:

http://www.hotwired.com/wired/ 3.07/features/dawkins.html

3.08

Design: John Brockman's critique of the literary establishment was symbolized by the imagery chosen by Erik Adigard.

Quote: John Brockman, a high-octane literary agent and author of *By the Late John Brockman* and *The Third Culture*.

Imagery: Erik Adigard/MAD

Story:

http://www.hotwired.com/wired/ 3.08/features/brockman.html

3.09

Design: We contrasted an old group photo of workers forming the American flag with a video feed of the battered federal building in Oklahoma to symbolize Jon Katz's contention that America's public spaces have gone from being places of consensus to battle grounds.

Quote: Jon Katz, a media critic and former executive producer of the CBS Evening News.

Imagery: Alfred P. Murrah Federal Building: Bill Nation/Sygma Photo News; American flag: Brent Clingman

Story:

http://www.hotwired.com/wired/3.09/features/oj.html

3.10

Design: The designers Adams/Morioka created nearly a symbol-per-word story to illustrate Hans Moravec's belief that fully auto-mated industry will lead to life-time retirement.

Quote: Hans Moravec, a professor at Carnegie Mellon University's Robotics Institute.

Imagery: Adams/Morioka

Story:

http://www.hotwired.com/wired/3.10/features/moravec.html

3.11

Design: Po Bronson's descriptions of entrepreneurs as women and of venture capitalists as roosters was brought literally and eerily to life by 3-D illustrator Steve Speer.

Quote: Po Bronson, the best-selling author of *Bombardiers*.

Imagery: Steven Speer

Story:

http://www.hotwired.com/wired/3.11/features/vc.html

3.12

Design: We used a ticker-tape and stock photos of different types of markets and sellers from around the world to amplify Mark Andreessen's thoughts about the Net as the ultimate free-market economy, where individuals can have as strong a voice as organiza-tions. These are followed by the electrical image of a livestock fair in Rajastan State, India.

Quote: Marc Andreessen, co-founder of and vice president of technology at Netscape Communications Corporation.

Imagery: First Spread: Kowloon, Hong Kong: Telegraph Color Library/FPG; Billings, Montana: Nicholoas deVore III/Bruce Coleman; Sierra Leone: Pedro Coll/Stock Market; Singapore: Toyohiro Yamada/FPG; Aknolonga, Guatemala: Thomas Hoepker/Magnum; Tokyo: Ben Simmons/Stock Market; Chichicatenango, Guatemala: Thomas Hoepker/Magnum; New York: Richard Laird/FPG
Second Spread: Aksu, China: Bossan/Contrasto/SABA; Tel Aviv: Andy Hernandez/Sipa; Istanbul: Marvullo/Stock Market; New York: Brad Rickerby/Sipa; Varanasi, India: Jean Kugler/FPG; Tokyo: Ric Ergenbright; Meknes, Morocco: Gruyart/Magnum; Guangzhou, China: Sinopex/Rea/SABA; Chicago: Ralf-Finn Hestoft/SABA; Shanghai, China: Dan Habib/Impact Visuals; Oaxaca, Mexico: Bruce Stadder/FPG; Bozeman, Montana: David Madison/Bruce Coleman; Venice, California: Carolina Kroon/Impact Visuals; Beijing: Adrian Bradshaw/SABA; Phnom Penh, Cambodia: Leah Melnick/Impact Visuals; Califor-nia: Costa Manos/Magum; USSR: Masha Nordbye/Bruce Coleman; Varanasi, India: Jean Kugler/FPG; Rajasthan, India: Jean Kugler/FPG; Tokyo: Rene Burri/Magnum; Beijing: Dan Hibb/Impact Visuals; Ghardaia, Algeria: J. C. Carton/Bruce Coleman; Bridgetown, Barbados: Tony Arruza/Bruce Coleman; Amsterdam: Tony Arruza/Bruce Coleman
Third Spread: Nicholoas deVore III/Bruce Coleman

Story:

http://www.hotwired.com/wired/3.12/features/andreessen.html

Colophon

Mind Grenades: Manifestos from the Future was designed and produced digitally. Our thanks to the makers of the following:

Hardware

Apple Macintosh Quadra and Power Macintosh personal computers, PowerBook Duos and Duo Docks, Work Group Servers; Portrait Pivot 1700 Displays; Radius Precision Color Displays, Precision Color Calibrators, Video-Vision, PhotoBooster, Thunder IV graphics cards; Apple LaserWriter 16/600, Dataproducts LZR 1580 laser printers; Hewlett-Packard LaserJet 4MV; Tektronix Phaser 480 color printer; Nikon Coolscan 35-mm film scanner; UMax UC 1260 flatbed scanner; APS storage media; MicroNet DAT backup and 1- and 2-Gbyte drives; Pinnacle Micro Sierra 1.3-Gbyte magneto-optical drive; Global Village TelePort Gold modems, Supra FaxModems.

Software

Page layout and illustration: QuarkXPress, Quark Publishing System; Adobe Illustrator, Dimensions, Photoshop, and Streamline; Kai's Power Tools and Xaos Tools Paint Alchemy Photoshop plug-ins; Electric Image Animation System; Macromedia Fontographer; WordPerfect.

Typography

Cover typeface: Warehouse, by House Industries.

Text: Adobe Myriad and Wiredbaum (designed for *Wired* by Matthew Carter).

Heds: Adobe, FontShop, [T-26], House Industries, FUSE.

Graphics support

Aldus Fetch; Equilibrium Technologies DeBabelizer; Adobe Premiere.

Networking: Apple Remote Access; CE Software QuickMail; Dantz Retrospect Remote; Engage Communication ISDN Express Router; Farallon Timbuktu Pro; Qualcomm Eudora; Shiva LanRover/E Plus; StarNine Internet Gateway; Xinet; Unix weenie documentation: O'Reilly & Assoc., Inc.

Electronic prepress

Danbury Printing & Litho, Danbury, Connecticut, a subsidiary of Banta Corp.

Color separations

are made on a DS America 608 scanner linked directly to a Scitex MacCSS system. Preliminary color corrections are performed on a Scitex PrisMagic and proofed on the paper stock using a Kodak Approval digital color-proofing system. Additional electronic prepress is performed in-house at *Wired* and HardWired using scans from the DS America 608, UMax UC 1260, Nikon Coolscan, and Kodak PhotoCD. Composed pages are converted to PostScript through a PS2 and translated into Scitex language using software version 4.12. RIP'd files are sent to the Scitex Micro Assembler and PrisMagic workstations. Composed digital proofs are submitted for final approval. Final film is plotted on a Scitex Dolev 800.

Printing

Tien Wah Press (pte.) Ltd, Singapore

Paper

Cover: Ensogloss Artboard c2s

Text: Nymolla Matte Art